Praise for *The Tibetan Book of the Dead for Beginners*

"Lama Lhanang Rinpoche and Mordy Levine have written a gracious, elegant book that illuminates the renowned *Tibetan Book of the Dead* in simple yet profound language perfectly tailored for contemporary readers. They uncover the wisdom of the great Tibetan enlightened master Padmasambhava's teachings on how to live, how to approach inevitable death, and how to help loved ones facing death. Both new and experienced practitioners will find this book provides an opportunity for transformation and growth."

ORGYEN CHOWANG RINPOCHE
author of *Our Pristine Mind*

"*The Tibetan Book of the Dead for Beginners* is an absolute treasure. It is a thorough, concise introduction to the classic work. It contains practical guidance on what to expect and how to care for loved ones and one's self at the time of transition."

BRIDGETTE SHEA, LAc, MAcOM
author of *Handbook of Chinese Medicine and Ayurveda*

"*The Tibetan Book of the Dead* is a profound Buddhist text. It offers us a timeless wisdom that guides on how to live with joy and die with peace. This new book elucidates this ancient text in clear, contemporary language that makes it practical and applicable for people today. May it bring about insight into a deeper meaning of life to whoever reads it."

ANAM THUBTEN
author of *Choosing Compassion*

T0035262

"This book is a practical beginners' guide that prepares all of us—no matter what culture or religion, at home or in hospital—for the eventual dying process. Personal intention and practice to develop wisdom and compassion in life are keys to dying as we have lived. In our dying process we can create good karma moving forward with our evolving consciousness."

DR. LOBSANG DHONDUP
founder and director of Tibetan Healing Center

"This is a joyful book, offering an option to not shy away from the natural process of dying while remembering to celebrate every moment of life along the way. May its merits pervade everywhere."

AL ZOLYNAS
Zen teacher

"An accessible book that offers many practical suggestions to those supporting those dying and to those who are dying themselves. I especially appreciated the section on cultivating compassion, which necessarily includes self-compassion."

BOB ISAACSON
cofounder, president, and CEO of Dharma Voices for Animals

THE
TIBETAN
BOOK OF
THE DEAD
FOR
BEGINNERS

THE
TIBETAN
BOOK OF
THE DEAD
FOR
BEGINNERS

A Guide to Living and Dying

Lama Lhanang Rinpoche | Mordy Levine

sounds true
BOULDER, COLORADO

Sounds True
Boulder, CO 80306

Published 2023

Cover design by Jennifer Miles
Book design by Meredith Jarrett

Printed in the United States of America

BK06726

Library of Congress Cataloging-in-Publication Data

Names: Lama Lhanang, Rinpoche, author. | Levine, Mordy, author.
Title: The Tibetan book of the dead for beginners : a guide to living and
  dying / Lama Lhanang Rinpoche and Mordy Levine.
Description: Boulder : Sounds True, 2023.
Identifiers: LCCN 2022036609 (print) | LCCN 2022036610 (ebook) | ISBN
  9781649631329 (trade paperback) | ISBN 9781649631336 (ebook)
Subjects: LCSH: Intermediate state—Buddhism. | Death—Religious
  aspects—Buddhism. | Buddhist funeral rites and ceremonies.
Classification: LCC BQ4490 .L36 2023 (print) | LCC BQ4490 (ebook) | DDC
  294.3/423—dc23/eng/20221013
LC record available at https://lccn.loc.gov/2022036609
LC ebook record available at https://lccn.loc.gov/2022036610

10 9 8 7 6 5 4 3 2 1

FSC
www.fsc.org
MIX
Paper | Supporting
responsible forestry
FSC® C103098

"The past is history. The future is mystery.
The present moment is a gift."

—LAMA LHANANG RINPOCHE

Dedication

May all beings have happiness and
the causes of happiness.
May all beings be free from suffering
and the causes of suffering.
May all beings rejoice in the wellbeing of others.
May all beings live in peace, free
from greed and hatred.

—THE FOUR IMMEASURABLES

Contents

Acknowledgments

W e wish to express our great appreciation to those who helped this book come to fruition: Khandro Tsering Choeden, Maricruz Gomez, Alberto Garcia, Cynthia Orozco, Tom Seidman, Elizabeth Levine, Richard Harmon, Sondra Harmon, Catherine Scrivens, Sarah Stanton, and Joe Kulin.

Introduction

No one knows when our end will come. Whether we die alone or with loved ones, unexpectedly or after a long illness, after a long life or a shorter one, many people appear to be ill-prepared for the time of death.

As we wrote this book, the COVID-19 pandemic raged around the world. Millions of people have died worldwide—more than one million in the United States, where we live, with many people dying alone in hospitals without the comfort of family, friends, and loved ones by their side.

The COVID-19 pandemic offers a poignant reminder that it doesn't matter what our religion is, or our economic status, or our viewpoints on any matter. In the end, we are all the same. No one wants suffering. We are all born. We will all die.

In most contemporary Western cultures, if death is discussed at all, it comes in hushed voices. We shield ourselves and our children from any meaningful discussion of the end of life or what happens after. Death is feared, and speaking of it creates discomfort. It is rarely discussed openly.

Western medicine and technology improve our health and can be lifesavers during critical times. Unfortunately, they are sometimes used to push death away, at the cost of unnecessary emotional suffering by the patient and family.

In most contemporary Eastern cultures, senior citizens live within the community, and within the home of their family. As they age, they are respected, supported, and still a part of the community and family fabric. They live at home and die at home, in the bosom of their family and community.

Western culture today tends to hide our seniors away in nursing homes or senior living centers—where we can visit them periodically. They are left to navigate the end of their lives with professional caretakers. Families rush in for the final lap, often feeling fear, stress, great emotion, and little sense of how to accommodate or support their loved one.

Regardless of how and where we live our final years, and whether we see death coming or not, it will touch us all. But we don't have to be afraid.

How We Die

The death process is different for every one of us. There is no formula for how someone "should" die, or what a "good" death even means. Each death is unique, and what is appropriate for one person or family may not be for another. The manner in which we die and how those around us deal with it is truly unique. The following stories illustrate how differently we can all experience our death or the death of our loved ones.

INTENSIVE CARE

Mom came to the intensive care unit three weeks ago in the middle of the night. Who could have predicted or prepared for this? Small and weak, she is aware of her surroundings but unable to speak.

She becomes weaker each day. From our conversations with her over the years we know her desire was to spend her last days at home. Now Mom is surrounded with beeping machines, tubes, and medical personnel. She is hooked up to machines, without which she would certainly not live. We all know her days are numbered. We want to make sure that she dies peacefully without any physical or emotional pain. How can we do that now?

AT HOME

My husband had been keeping himself alive for years despite his prognosis—with medication, meditation, and gentle exercise. Death, once years away, had crept up on us and became only weeks away. We slowed down our daily routines and switched gears to make sure my husband would pass away in peace and quiet, surrounded by loved ones and the music and art he loved so much. One day, after we had finished a recitation of his favorite poetry, his eyes closed. We knew that wherever his spirit or consciousness went, he was happy, content, and with no regrets.

SUDDEN LOSS

Our sister always ran around at warp speed in everything she did. From when she was a toddler until her thirty-second birthday, she was determined to achieve and do everything she possibly could at breakneck speed—regardless of what was in front of her or was left in her wake. Her car accident was just an extension of how she led her life. One instant she was our sister, the live wire—and then she wasn't. We learned from the police report that she was conscious for a few hours before eventually dying from a severe concussion. We never had a chance to say goodbye, or tell her how much we loved her.

These experiences are sobering. And if you haven't been with someone who is dying, we can assure you that living through these moments is more intense and prolonged than you could ever imagine. This is reality.

We are very fortunate that with the expansion of hospice care, our loved ones can die with love and compassion. We can learn so much from the hospice care angels who care for our loved ones at the end of life.

Is it possible that death can be a celebratory and empowering event? Is it possible to enjoy our lives and, as a result, be better prepared for death as it approaches? *What if death can truly become part of the cycle of life?*

The Tibetan Book of the Dead for Beginners shares ancient wisdom on death from the perspective of Tibetan Buddhism, made accessible for readers today—whether Buddhist or not. By learning to acknowledge the reality of death, we can live more fully, die with more peace, and support our loved ones in doing the same. In this book, we hope to share this promise with you.

A Tibetan Buddhist View of Death

Buddhism is well equipped to prepare us for death. Buddhists know that how we live is how we will die. In Tibetan Buddhism, the prospect of death is acknowledged in daily practices, prayers, and teachings that motivate us to live an ethical and happy life. And living with joy and kindness allows us to approach death with confidence and ease.

Buddhists aspire for death to be a smooth, natural, and peaceful process, as we transition into our next post-life experience. To achieve this takes practice while we are alive—practice in the form of meditation, contemplation, and skillful action under the guidance of a qualified Buddhist Master.

If you study death, it can be a transforming, liberating event. If you don't, it can be very difficult emotionally.

The Dalai Lama's Thoughts on Death

His Holiness the 14th Dalai Lama frequently addresses death in his teaching. He writes:

> As a Buddhist, I view death as a normal process, a reality that I accept will occur as long as I remain in this earthly existence. Knowing that I cannot escape it, I see no point in worrying about it. I tend to think of death as being like changing your clothes when they are old and worn out, rather than as some final end. Yet death is unpredictable: We do not know when or how it will take place. So it is only sensible to take certain precautions before it actually happens.

The Dalai Lama prepares himself for the time of death, and as a result does not worry about it. We concur wholeheartedly with his view that we can prepare for it, and in that preparation, we can learn to accept it as well. And in this book, we will show you how we can work with our state of mind now, how to live a meaningful life, and, at the time of death, how to bring about a happy rebirth.

The Tibetan Book of the Dead

Among the numerous Buddhist texts that address the end of life, one of the most widely read, taught, and discussed is *The Tibetan Book of the Dead*. Scholars believe it was composed in the eighth century by the great Buddhist Master Padmasambhava and then discovered in central Tibet in the fourteenth century.

The text describes practices that prepare the Buddhist practitioner for the experience that awaits us from the time we start to die until we are reborn. As we become more accomplished in this preparation, our level of confidence while alive and as we prepare for death increases. Through these practices, we also experience a sense of calm, compassion, and wisdom.

When we are able to include the practices described by this great master in our daily lives, the prospect of death can be viewed as an empowering opportunity.

Lama Lhanang has taught the practices in *The Tibetan Book of the Dead* to countless people around the world, and he has witnessed the powerful impact of these teachings in their lives—and in the lives of their loved ones. The full text of *The Tibetan Book of the Dead* is widely available, but to a reader who isn't an advanced Buddhist practitioner the book can feel esoteric and inaccessible. This book draws on the concepts shared in *The Tibetan Book of the Dead* to make the teachings available to anyone who is curious about them, to anyone courageous enough to live life fully and prepare for its end.

Appendix A shares a brief summary of the kinds of practices found in *The Tibetan Book of the Dead*, but you won't find its full original text in this book. Instead, you will find teachings drawn from its heart, tested across generations and continents, and offered with the intention to ease suffering and bring more joy and peace.

The Tibetan Book of the Dead provides us with a description of all the phases that human beings experience in the birth-life-death-afterlife cycle. It introduces the concept of Buddha nature—the basic and fundamental nature of all sentient beings. And finally, the great Master Padmasambhava introduces many visualizations, prayers, and practices that advanced practitioners can use to guide a dying person through the process of death and the afterlife to ensure their consciousness has an auspicious rebirth, or goes to the Pure Land.

We offer this beginner's book on Buddhist practices and teachings on life and death, based on *The Tibetan Book of the Dead*, so that anyone who is interested can achieve calmness and confidence as death approaches them or a loved one.

And, as importantly, anyone can utilize these teachings to be happier while they are alive. This book is written to guide us to live our lives joyfully. The natural result will then be for us to die peacefully.

It is our wish that this book will provide access to these precious teachings and practices to people of all religions. After all, in the events of life and death, we are all the same.

As the Dalai Lama says, "When I see people with smiles, I feel these are all my brothers, sisters; seven billion human beings, actually, our brothers and sisters."

We hope this book is of great benefit to you and your loved ones.

Chapter 1

Karma—How We Live Is How We Die

"If a person speaks or acts with a
pure thought, happiness follows, like
a shadow that never leaves."

—BUDDHA, FROM THE DHAMMAPADA

You don't need to be a Buddhist to believe in karma, also known as the Law of Cause and Effect.

How we speak or act at this moment determines our experience in the next moment. How we live today impacts how we live tomorrow, the next day, the next week, month, year—and, when you believe in rebirth, in our future lives.

If we love unconditionally, love will come to us. When the flower grows, the bees and butterflies all come and enjoy it. When we open our heart, everyone wants to be near. When we close our heart, no one wants to be around us.

Karma does not lie, and we can't run away from it. If you really want to know your karma, look at yourself in the mirror. How we are now results from what we have done in our life until now. Our karma in the future is determined by what we are thinking, doing, and saying now.

How Karma Works

Many books and teachings are devoted to explaining the complex nature of karma. And understanding karma is invaluable in seeing the relationship between the present moment and the end of life.

Our actions result in consequences. And when we speak of *action* we refer to physical action, speech, or thought.

The consequences that we will experience come in the form of creating a habit of our actions. In the future, we will find ourselves in the same kinds of environments where the actions initially occurred. And finally, we will become the recipient of those actions, as well.

Habitual consequences relate to our mindset and actions. Environmental consequences relate to our surroundings. And personal consequences relate to our circumstances.

Here are a few examples:

If we are generous with someone, then three consequences may follow:

1. We will be generous again in the future (habitual consequence).
2. We will find ourselves in an environment where people are generous (environmental consequence).
3. We will be the recipient of someone else's generosity in the future (personal consequence).

If right now our colleague or loved one speaks to us in a way that triggers our anger, then these three consequences may follow:

1. We will be angry in a similar situation in the future (habitual consequence).
2. We will find ourselves in an environment where those around us are angry (environmental consequence).
3. We will find ourselves in a situation where others are angry with us (personal consequence).

Every thought, speech, or action that we take as a reaction to what happens to us or around us creates karma, a consequence.

Our intention precedes or triggers our thoughts, speech, or actions. Intention is the basis of karma. Good intention yields good karma, and vice versa.

As we change our inner world—through thought, speech, and action—the external world around us reflects those changes.

When We Experience Karma

When does one experience the results of one's actions? When does karma come to fruition?

We experience the "fruits" of our actions anytime from the very next moment to years or lifetimes later.

Let's use the analogy of planting a vegetable seed in a field. When does it ripen? And how good will it taste?

Well, that depends on many variables. Here are just a few—sun, earth, fertilizer, water, how much sun, how much water, when it was planted, if it was a big seed, if it was a small seed, how many seeds, what the ground was like, the season when it was planted.

These are but a few of the variables that determine the result of the seed being planted.

Karma *seeds* that are in your mind, likewise, sometimes ripen immediately and sometimes in the future. The future for most Buddhists includes this lifetime, as well as future lifetimes.

How We Work with Karma

From a Tibetan Buddhist perspective, we have the ability to purify our negative karma. In other words, we can work to mitigate the negative consequences of past negative actions. Purification practices are an important focus of chanting and prayers in Tibetan schools of Buddhism. They include meditation, an admission or confession of the actions that created the negative karma, remorse, and intention not to commit the actions that caused the negative karma again in the future. Although we can read about these practices or watch videos about them, Tibetan Buddhist purification practices are best learned directly from a qualified teacher.

Even if we haven't learned these traditional practices, we can dilute our negative karma—just by engaging in more positive actions, and fewer actions that create negative karma.

As mentioned earlier, what we experience now in life is a result of all of our actions until this moment. And likewise, how we deal with circumstances around us now determines our future. So, in a sense, from this moment on, we all create our own karma!

With that in mind, many of us use karma to attribute blame to ourselves or others. This can be counterproductive, and in many cases not true. The best example of this is blaming individuals or groups of people today for what they may or may not have done in previous lifetimes. We can only hold ourselves accountable for actions that we took in this lifetime. Identifying actions that may have been taken by an individual in previous lifetimes is almost impossible to do, and can only cause harm.

We must look at what we can control—the present and the future. Our future is not predetermined. We determine it.

To quote the Buddha from the Dhammapada: "You yourselves must strive; the Buddhas only point the way."

We are planting karma *seeds* in our field of consciousness with every action we take, and those seeds mature at different rates, with different strengths, and in different ways. Our intention, and the strength of it, is the basis of karma.

Also, we don't have a single independent karma account, like a bank account with a running balance.

We've got lots of karma accounts at different stages of development. All we can see at any one moment are the seeds that are currently sprouting. As for the other seeds that haven't yet sprouted—good or bad—we can't see those at all. They sprout at different rates and times, and interact with each other, as well.

Once again, it is not just physical actions that create karma. Actions include those of the body, speech, and mind.

If our intentions are full of friendliness, that will generate good karma. If our mind's intentions are selfish and full of pride, then that will generate negative karma.

We develop habits of body, speech, and mind that we continue to reinforce—until we break the habit.

Each day that we continue with our habits reinforces the habits the next day. If we are a generous, kind person today, and create a habit of these actions, those habits stay with us tomorrow and the next day. That chain reaction continues until the moment we die—and, as we shall see, after death as well.

The key to transforming our life is what we do in this moment—now.

Chapter 2

What Dies and What Gets Reborn

Does our body die? Clearly.

What about our brain? That clearly dies too.

What about our personality, our soul, our spirit, our identity, our sense of self?

Before we talk about death and rebirth, we need to know what is dying. And for those who believe in rebirth, what is getting reborn.

The Self

Let's start by examining this thing that we call the "self."

Here is a working definition of the self:

The self is who we think we are, based on the stories we tell ourselves. We develop, nurture, protect, and prop up our identity with stories about ourselves and the world around us.

A common question in Buddhism, and many religions and philosophies, is, "Does the self exist?"

And the Buddhist answer is, "Yes, it does, but not in the way we think or act."

The self is not a permanent solid "I" or "me." It is a constantly changing sense of who we think we are—from moment to moment and from day to day. It is not a fixed, concrete entity.

Many religions believe in a soul—a permanent, eternal, unchanging, underlying essence. Buddhism does not. In fact, the Buddha himself never said one way or the other that the self exists or doesn't exist.

When the Buddha started teaching the concept of karma, he viewed ideas of "self" and "not-self" as types of karma.

He defined the creation and support of our sense of self—the habitual telling of stories about ourselves—as an action. An action creates karma.

Being generous is an action that creates karma. Being mean or cruel creates karma. Likewise, how we develop our identity or sense of self is karma that we create as well.

The question becomes, under what circumstances does the action of developing your "self" create positive or negative karma?

Our Selves and Our Karma

Here are three examples that illustrate how karma is created based on how we view and support our "self."

SENSE OF SELF WITH FAMILY
John views himself as a good father and a good husband. He is convinced that he is and takes great pride in himself. The stories

that he tells himself about being a good father or husband support that aspect of his self-identity.

But his wife and son do not see him as a good father or a good husband after he yells at them. This creates an ongoing conflict in the family, with all family members holding on to their views strongly.

The more John grasps and holds on to the concept that he is a good father or husband, the more attached he is to this aspect of his sense of "self," and the more negative karma he creates. If John is open-minded about who he thinks he is, and is able to consider other perspectives in this regard, he creates positive karma. For example, maybe he can be a better father. Maybe he has had too narrow a view of himself in this regard. Maybe he just has a different view of himself than others—in which case, what makes his view right and someone else's view wrong?

SENSE OF SELF IN OUR CAREER

Sumi has her dream job as a surgeon in a hospital where she has worked for ten years. She loves it. It is part of her being. The strong view of her "self" is intertwined with her career as a surgeon. In the medical field, many doctors or nurses see their occupation as a "calling."

One day, Sumi visited a patient after surgery and was very abrupt in her manner. Her patient was very upset and told others that Sumi was a horrible physician. Sumi was extremely upset and angry. Her patient's view was in direct conflict with the strong beliefs Sumi had of herself and her identity.

If Sumi is open to the possibility that she was not the best physician she could have been at that moment, she is creating positive karma. If Sumi is absolutely 100 percent sure that everything she did was perfect and leaves no room for improvement, that would create negative karma.

The grasping to support a strong sense of self-identity creates negative karma. Considering alternative views of the "self" loosens that grasping of self-identity and creates positive karma.

We can be open to all possibilities and all opinions of ourselves—without taking offense. We can be free to change our own opinions of ourselves as we gather more information. We can have opinions of ourselves and others of course, but we don't want to hold on too tightly to them—because we would be factualizing something illusory and subject to change. Holding on tightly to who we think we are only sets us up for failure and disappointment, especially when we are faced with another differing opinion.

SENSE OF SELF IN SOCIAL SETTINGS

Jose is nervous in social environments, and it causes him anxiety. Jose tells himself stories (true or false) over and over again about how he thinks he is (or should be) in social environments. The action of creating these stories supports his view of himself.

The more Jose believes the self-dialogue of "I am a shy, private person that doesn't do well around people," the more he is grasping on to his sense of self.

The more Jose grasps, the more resistance arises when it is time to go to, or avoid, social engagements. This is an example of negative karma being created.

The degree of conflict Jose feels, or the strength of his reaction to what happens around him, is a reflection of how strong his sense of self is.

Jose doesn't like this about himself and decides to change his life. He starts to attend small gatherings of only two to three people. He vows to speak more in one-on-one conversations. He seeks help with a professional to overcome his fear. Regardless of his success, all of these sincere efforts create good karma.

SENSE OF SELF WHEN DEALING WITH FEAR

Mari is afraid of heights but continues to work on reducing that fear. By doing so, Mari weakens her sense of self, and moves away from identifying herself as someone who is afraid. She starts on her own by looking out a window on the second floor of her work environment. Then a week later, she opens the window to see what is outside. She works with a friend to walk in and then out of an elevator. As she improves in these micro-steps, she gains confidence. She still is afraid, but she sees what she is able to achieve on her own. She seeks professional help to continue to work on reducing or overcoming this fear. This is an example of creating positive karma.

If Mari didn't work on that fear, or if she let it continue or worsen, that would strengthen her identity in this regard. This is an example of creating negative karma.

And, of course, this aspect of Mari's self-identity is formed and would strengthen by the myriad of stories that she uses to tell herself about this fear. Now those stories are weaker, less true, and are not such a concrete part of her self-identity.

Working with Our Sense of Self

How we view and strengthen (or weaken) our sense of self creates karma.

We can measure our degree of grasping when we look at how strong our tendencies or habits are.

We can measure how strong these habits are by how much internal resistance we feel when something happens that doesn't fit our view of our "self."

Look at how we react to what happens to us or around us. A strong reaction to support our sense of self creates negative karma.

Look at the triggers that create a negative state of mind. A strong reaction to those triggers is indicative of the increased attachment to our self-identity. The stronger we support our self-identity, the greater the negative karma.

The good news is, since we create our "self" and our habits, we can also control them.

Our Selves, Our Karma

We return to the question: "What gets reborn?"

What is reborn is our consciousness that contains our karmic impressions, or our ingrained habits. The karmic seeds we create are like impressions in our consciousness, a type of memory.

Our consciousness contains our sense of self. It is a type of memory or impression that continues on after we die.

Here are some common situations when we grasp and tell ourselves stories to support our identity—which creates karma.

How much we judge ourselves or hold on to our perspective determines whether the karma we create is negative or positive.

- fear of heights
- attachment to money
- grasping at fame
- self-importance
- aversion to social engagements
- fear of failure
- fear of intimacy

How we grasp (or not) in these situations creates impressions that get strengthened (negative karma) or weakened (positive karma) in our consciousness. For every fear or every "fact" we "know" about ourselves there is a way to see that it is just not true.

To quote Mark Twain: "It ain't what you don't know that gets you into trouble. It's what you know for sure that just ain't so."

Here are examples of antidotes, in the form of small steps for how one might reduce their attachment to these views of themselves:

Attachment to money—donate small amounts to charities that you would like to support. Give any amount of money to a person experiencing homelessness.

Grasping at fame, self-importance—volunteer at a shelter for unhoused people, or for animals, or at a hospital, or with any group less fortunate than you.

Fear of failure—find an activity you like to do and don't keep score. Set a goal of just doing it without an end goal in mind. Just by doing the activity, you have achieved your goal. Over time you learn to appreciate the activity and not the end result.

These micro-steps may not be easy. They may be very difficult, in fact. We are breaking down and stripping away the views we have had of ourselves our whole life. But it is a worthwhile and noble effort.

There is no one right answer for how we begin to relax our views of ourselves, but starting anywhere, starting now, and starting in small doses are always good places to begin. And of course, professional help can always be supportive.

The consciousness containing these impressions is what continues after our body and brain die—and eventually is reborn in a new body. While we live, reducing our fears gives us freedom and confidence. This is invaluable. And as we approach death, we have the confidence that our consciousness is not filled with the karmic seeds of our fears or anxieties. We have created beneficial habits. We are open-minded. We know the world is ever changing—impermanent and illusory—not something to solidify. We are open to seeing ourselves through many different lenses. And as we learn to live with that open-mindedness, we are less likely to feel afraid or anxious. We can work with or deal with what comes our way with greater patience and even joy.

Chapter 3

Our Consciousness after Death

When we die our physical body returns to nature. Death is a natural part of the cycle of life. We are born, so we must die.

Like a flower that grows into beauty, after it dies, its seeds grow, continuing the flower's life cycle. Similarly, after we die, our consciousness continues onto its next phase.

As mentioned earlier, our habits (karma) are embedded in our consciousness and continue on. Some scientists now agree with Buddhists who believe that our consciousness continues after we die. People who have had a taste of their death and afterlife have shared their experiences. And based on their experience they are no longer afraid of death. It is just another part of our life cycle, and even something they look forward to when they approach death again. They are our witnesses, our front runners, and our guides to what is possible for us after death.

The Moments after Death

Let's start with the immediate moments after death—defined medically as when the heart stops beating, which results in immediate cessation of brain activity.

There are numerous documented stories of people who have experienced death and come back to life within minutes. These are termed "near-death experiences" (NDEs).

Common NDEs include when the deceased person:

- hears and sees people as their consciousness floats above their body
- sees light at the end of a tunnel
- experiences a review of their lifetime's memories
- sees a god figure

Many people who experience an NDE describe feeling a certain relief after they die and their consciousness exits their body. Many experiences include seeing golden light and/or luminous beings.

And although it is beyond the scope of this book to detail these NDEs, we know that after the brain and body cease to work, awareness continues, as documented in thousands of the NDE cases.

In addition to these profound experiences, great saints and meditation masters of many faiths tell of their consciousness maintaining awareness after their body has been dead for days, or in some cases weeks, before coming back to life.

The Bardos

What about the vast majority of those who die and do not return to their body, those who remain dead? From a Buddhist perspective, the consciousness experiences an intermediate, transition-like state until it is reborn in a new body.

The experiences in this state, or period of time until rebirth, are known as the Intermediate State, or the *bardo*. The English translation for the bardo, appropriately enough, is "gap."

The Tibetan Book of the Dead not only describes what happens to us when we die—it also details what we can do to improve our experience in the bardo and prepare for a good rebirth.

Bardo can also describe any gap in one's life. For example, the term *bardo* can be used to refer to a pause between breaths, a vacation, a pandemic year, or a time of change or transition.

Tibetan Buddhist lineages map our life cycle in terms of six bardos (time periods). The first three bardos relate to while we are alive, as follows:

1. *Bardo of this Life*—The time period of our lives as we are experiencing it now.
2. *Bardo of the Dream State*—The time period when we are asleep and dreaming.
3. *Bardo of Meditation*—The time period when we are meditating.

The last three bardos refer to the time periods between death and rebirth:

4. *Bardo of Dying*—The time period when our body is in the process of dying. All the physical elements of

our body dissolve, and only pure awareness remains. During this period our mind can become very clear and can recall all of our past positive and negative actions. We feel at peace as we remember the positive actions, and fearful as we recall the negative actions.

5. *Bardo of Luminosity*—Our body and brain are dead. We experience visionary and auditory sensations—not unlike the dream state while sleeping when we are alive. This can include the appearance of ghosts, demons, gods, as well as a judge of our karmic account—all created by our state of mind. There can also be a "feeling" of peace and heartfelt, intense awareness.

6. *Bardo of Becoming*—The time between when our consciousness (karma) enters the mother's womb until the time we are reborn. Entry into the mother's womb results from the habit of the consciousness to grasp for a physical body for its identity, or a sense of self.

As in *The Tibetan Book of the Dead*, this book focuses especially on the fourth, fifth, and sixth bardos, given our desire to prepare ourselves for death and what comes after this life.

The Fifth Bardo

Tibetan Buddhist lineages teach that our consciousness can be in the fifth bardo for up to forty-nine days. As mentioned earlier, while in the fifth bardo, we experience a variety of phenomena, some similar to the dream state we experience while asleep during this lifetime. As we all know, during the dream state, we can experience happy dreams, nightmares, and everything imaginable in between.

Buddhist teachings share that while we are asleep our dreams are a reflection of our state of mind. For example, if prior to going to sleep we watch a happy uplifting movie, we are more likely to have happy dreams. If prior to sleep we have a very difficult or stressful day at work, or an argument with a loved one, we are more likely to have a negative dream experience.

When we discussed karma, we saw that each moment impacts the next moment in our lives. Just as our moments prior to sleeping impact our dream state, our moments prior to death also impact our experience in the bardo.

Our dreams are also impacted by how we live our life. Our karmic tendencies impact our dreams as well. If we are angry, that will be reflected in our dreams, and vice versa. If we are constantly grasping for financial gain, power, sex, or love, that tendency influences our experience in dreaming.

Dream yoga practitioners are individuals who practice awareness while dreaming, and are able to control their dream experience. The training for this skill includes meditation practices that enable us to control our states of mind when awake, as well as when asleep.

The skills practiced in dream yoga help the practitioner navigate and influence the experience in the fifth bardo, Bardo of Luminosity. We will discuss some of these meditation practices in the next chapters.

How we live our life—the karma we create—determines our state of mind prior to death, our experience in the bardo, and our rebirth.

Preparing for the Bardos

When we die, as mentioned earlier, our karmic habits, embedded in our consciousness, continue into the bardo. The degree of grasping and attachment, to maintain our self-importance, plays center stage for our consciousness in the bardo.

If we live with the aim to reduce our grasping and our fears, to practice kindness with others, and to understand that life is impermanent, then those efforts will be reflected positively in our consciousness as we enter the bardo. Our experiences in the bardo will not be nightmarish.

Our state of mind in the bardo similarly impacts the kind of rebirth we will have. One moment impacts the next—regardless of where we are in our continuum of the birth-life-death-rebirth cycle.

Chapter 4

Influencing Our Next Rebirth

Will we be reborn in a family that shows us love and compassion? Will we be reborn in a well-to-do city, or a poor, desolate neighborhood or country, or a country at war? Will we be reborn as a human or an animal? Do we even have a say in these matters?

Great Buddhist masters who have trained over many years (or lifetimes) are able to choose their family and location of rebirth. Before they die, many masters will go so far as to leave a letter and other information for their students as to where they will be reborn. This allows their students to find them after rebirth. The students search with the clues provided by their teacher. When they find a candidate who might be the rebirth of their teacher, they test the young child in a variety of ways to be certain the child is their former teacher. The child can now "continue" their Buddhist studies, and continue to work to reduce suffering for all sentient beings.

An inspiring movie to watch this take place is *Unmistaken Child*. A Buddhist monk, Tenzin Zopa, is tasked with finding his teacher, Geshe Lama Konchog, in his new incarnation.

The most well-known example of this cycle is the life of His Holiness the 14th Dalai Lama. As a child, he was identified, tested, and found to be the prior incarnation of His Holiness the 13th Dalai Lama.

How Buddhist Masters Navigate Rebirth

Through intense study and meditation, Buddhist masters train their minds to be compassionate and non-grasping, and they truly understand that the world is impermanent. Working with practices from *The Tibetan Book of the Dead* and other sources, they are prepared to navigate the bardo.

They are not fearful about death. They are able to control their states of mind while awake to avoid grasping, attachment, and fear. They maintain their awareness while asleep. And as they die, they are able to navigate the bardo with stability and awareness—the same way they lived their lives.

Great masters approach death the same way they live—with compassion for themselves and others. They have ceased, or reduced, their grasping of their "self."

How We Can Navigate Rebirth

Likewise, for us, how we live is how we will die. How we die is how we will experience the bardo. How we experience the bardo will be one of the ingredients that determine how and where we are reborn.

Most of us are not able to control our states of mind while awake or asleep. We grasp at the people, events, and things around us, and become attached to our desires or aversion to them. When our situation changes in a way we don't like, we experience stress, anger, annoyance, or irritation.

When we have good experiences, bad experiences, or nightmares, it seems like these things just happen to us. And we react based on our prior habitual reactions. We don't have the ability to control our reactive state of mind.

And if we are not able to control our minds during our waking hours, we will certainly not be able to be aware of, or control, our minds when we sleep, or are in the bardo. But we don't have to stay in these reactive states. We can learn to work with our minds so we can navigate our lives with more acceptance and prepare for death with more ease.

The way we live our life—which includes our level of awareness, degree of grasping, and other tendencies—is how we will experience the bardo. It is very important to be able to "let go" of our reactive grasping tendencies when in the bardo. We don't want to go through the bardo fighting the fears and demons that show up in our consciousness. After all, as we prepare for the bardo, we learn that our thoughts, perceptions, and views are an illusion. We no longer need to view ourselves, and what comes into our mind, with great solidity or importance.

In addition, the bardo experience is more difficult to navigate than the normal dream state we experience while alive.

For most of us, death can be a big shock to our consciousness, especially when it is sudden.

After death, many beings enter the bardo in a state of shock and resist the fact that they are dead. We see this resistance to death illustrated in movies such as *The Sixth Sense*, starring

Bruce Willis, or *Ghost* with Patrick Swayze, Demi Moore, and Whoopi Goldberg.

Some recently deceased cling to their former lives. Even while dead, they are aware of their family and friends who are still living and going about their lives. Family and friends who are agitated or arguing during or after the death event will impact the consciousness of our loved one in the bardo—and create agitation for the consciousness. If friends and family are able to maintain a sense of calm, peace, and love, that will allow the deceased to be more at peace while they continue through the bardo.

Consciousness Through the Bardo

Consciousness experiences the bardo without a physical body.

While alive, our physical body is very grounding for us.

When we get out of bed in the morning, when we exercise, when we pay attention to physical sensations, our physicality grounds us and helps our state of mind stabilize. For example, if we are stressed, we can take a walk or exercise our physical body. This helps to clear the physical, emotional, and psychological stress. Our mind-body connection is strong. What affects one impacts the other seamlessly.

When we meditate and observe our breath, we also connect our mind to our body.

While alive, our physical body in partnership with our mind interacts with the physical world around us, which is also grounding.

In the bardo we don't have our physical body to support us. We only have our consciousness—untethered from the body.

As mentioned earlier, in the bardo our consciousness includes our karma, the habits and tendencies that we have created, developed, and maintained through our lifetime(s).

If we are not able to control our states of mind while we are alive in our body, imagine how difficult it is after we die—when the mind is untethered from our physical body.

As we can see, navigating the bardo without preparation can be difficult. Our state of mind in the bardo mirrors our state of mind in this lifetime, without a body and in many cases in shock.

If we spent our lives grasping at desire and aversion, then the grasping to avoid fear and seeking for pleasure and comfort will play out in our experience in the bardo.

As mentioned in the previous chapter, at the end of the Bardo of Luminosity the grasping momentum of the consciousness, usually within forty-nine days, seeks to be in a body again. It seeks a womb, a physical body. And based on its karma, consciousness finds and enters a womb.

Karma determines our place of birth, family, and so on. For most beings, at this time in the cycle of life-death-rebirth, there is very little choice as to our rebirth environment. It is determined by our karma.

Can we prepare for the bardo—now that we know how much is riding on it?

We would all prefer to have a pleasant experience as we are dying. If we know the bardo experience is going to be unpleasant—or we are unprepared—we will live our lives in fear, and die in fear.

Appropriate preparation allows us to mentally relax to some degree. When we know what to expect and prepare our minds, we will feel more confident and peaceful as we approach the bardo.

Finally, from a very practical perspective, how we live our lives, including how we experience the bardo, determines our rebirth.

Let's prepare now while we can.

Chapter 5

Start Where We Are Now

Regardless of what transpires in life, regardless of our religion, regardless of our politics, our wealth, our good luck or bad luck, we know that our state of mind is:

- the only thing we can control
- the key to leading a life free of suffering, free of fear, and capable of dealing with whatever comes our way

This is not to say that everything in life is a bed of roses. The impermanence of life brings us sadness when our loved ones die, or when we hear of tragedies in our hometown or across the globe. But we can handle it. As we train our mind, we will have the tools to do so. And the uncertainty of life can also bring us joy!

The transforming of our mind aids us in approaching death with confidence and peace, so that death is a natural part of our lives.

The Buddha taught his followers to train their minds to reduce fear and grasping, which creates good karma, and to develop compassion for others, which reduces our permanent sense of self. For centuries, Buddhist practitioners have followed these methods, and today countless people practice them, whether Buddhist or not, because they experience benefits in their lives.

Mind training, through meditation, study, and prayer, reduces our suffering and improves our state of mind in this lifetime. At the same time, these activities help us prepare for the bardo experience when we die.

As we polish our mind to improve our experience in our current lifetime, our experience as we approach death, and in the bardo, will automatically improve.

More specifically, we can develop two critical ingredients to happiness in this lifetime, in the bardo, and in future lifetimes: compassion and wisdom.

Compassion

Compassion is the desire to reduce suffering for all beings. We learn to develop compassion for ourselves and for others— regardless of who they are and whether we like them or not.

How does this help us? As we develop compassion for others, we reduce our grasping and support of our own ego. They are two sides of the same coin.

When our mind looks at our situations with a focus on how it impacts "me" and "I," we automatically view ourselves as separate from others. We note differences and create judgments based on "me" versus "other." This mindset increases the support of our self-identity. And we know that as the grasping of our ego increases, we increase negative karma. More plainly, when our focus is primarily on ourselves, long-term inner happiness will never be ours.

Developing compassion creates good karma and reduces our sense of separateness, and in a direct sense we also feel better about ourselves. The impact of "me" and "I" thinking is weakened. In fact, our natural state of being contains a strong sense of compassion for others, as well as ourselves.

The Dalai Lama has spoken extensively about this topic: "When we feel love and kindness toward others, it not only makes others feel loved and cared for, but it helps us also to develop inner happiness and peace." He also says, "If you want others to be happy, practice compassion. If you want to be happy, practice compassion."

Developing a mind of compassion is a critical ingredient to our own happiness in this life. A mind of compassion is also a critical ingredient for when we experience the Bardo of Dying, the Bardo of Luminosity, and the Bardo of Becoming.

To paraphrase one lama—when you develop compassion in this lifetime, it is as if the universe rolls out the red carpet when you enter the bardo.

Practice Developing Compassion

There are many ways to develop compassion. One simple way is to recite, meditate, or contemplate a prayer called the Four Immeasurables.

The Four Immeasurables describes four attributes that we can develop for our self and others: lovingkindness, compassion, joy, and equanimity.

The prayer can be repeated numerous times as we contemplate its meaning:

May all beings have happiness and
the causes of happiness.
May all beings be free from suffering
and the causes of suffering.
May all beings rejoice in the wellbeing of others.
May all beings live in peace, free
from greed and hatred.

Line by line, it can be interpreted as follows:

- Lovingkindness is the desire that all of us are friendly toward each other and wish each other well.
- Compassion is the desire that all beings, including ourselves, not suffer.
- Joy is being happy for others' happiness and success.
- Equanimity means not being strongly attached to things we like, or strongly averse to things we don't like. We develop equanimity when we reduce our aversions and desires and strive to keep an even emotional keel. After all, everything always changes, so why grasp at something so strongly that inevitably will change.

We can also reflect on the prayer's meaning and study it until over time, little by little, we can feel it in our minds and live it in our lives.

Initially, while we repeat this prayer, we can hold our self and loved ones in our mind.

Over time, while we recite the prayer, we might incorporate those who we feel neutral about in our minds.

And eventually, while we recite the prayer, we might consider bringing into our mind people who we may not like or have not treated us well.

People err or make mistakes. We err and make mistakes. We certainly do not condone bad behavior. However, many people behave and act poorly as a result of an upbringing of abuse, or an environment that contributes to their behavior. We cannot pretend to know others' motivation when they cause harm or insult.

We do not condone their behavior, and we also do not wish suffering on them. By wishing harm on others, we harm ourselves and develop negative karma by doing so.

This shift in how we view others and ourselves moves us closer and closer to a life with reduced ego, less stress, and greater happiness. Grudges are forgotten, self-talk about the past or future—what "should have" or "might have" been—fades. This leaves us with a life enjoying and experiencing the present moment, as it is.

As we grow in this new and beautiful direction, we also see that we can be an active force in making the world a more beautiful and peaceful place. As we become more sensitive to the less fortunate, we feel compelled to help others. And with our evolving state of mind, we can use our actions of body, speech, and mind to bring peace and less suffering to those around us.

The development of compassion leads to a more peaceful death—a death with less worry, less stress, a better experience in the bardo, and, eventually, a more auspicious rebirth.

Additional practices that can incorporate a mind of compassion into our daily lives are found in appendix A.

Wisdom

Understanding wisdom is the second key ingredient to living a happy life. The development of wisdom also ensures a better experience in the bardo and future lifetimes.

Wisdom, as the Buddha taught, means seeing reality accurately—without illusions.

Earlier we asked, does our "self" exist? Yes and no. It exists—but not in the way we usually think. Our "self" is constantly changing and evolving. It does not have any permanent existence. We therefore say that the "self" is empty of inherent existence. The more we come to understand this over time—that our "self" is ever-changing and impermanent—the more we can feel and live with more freedom and liberation.

Not only is our "self" impermanent—everything is. All people, things, and situations change. Coming to understand impermanence can be painful, but it can also lead to freedom. This understanding helps us to reduce our grasping—after all, there is nothing solid to hold on to. Grasping at something that isn't there causes us suffering when reality splashes water in our face—and we find out we were chasing an illusion.

Impermanence also allows us to see how we are all inter-related. Change happens when something *causes* it to happen. Change does not happen *independently* of anything. The Law of Cause and Effect, karma, is another way of experiencing how we are all dependent and related to each other. All that happens to us is a result of something or someone.

Thich Nhat Hanh, the great Zen master, calls this phenomenon *interbeing*. As he so eloquently describes it:

Emptiness does not mean nothingness. Saying that we are empty does not mean that we do not exist. No matter if something is full or empty, that thing clearly needs to be there in the first place. When we say a cup is empty, the cup must be there in order to be empty. When we say that we are empty, it means that we must be there in order to be empty of a permanent, separate self.

About thirty years ago, I was looking for an English word to describe our deep interconnection with everything else. I liked the word "togetherness," but I finally came up with the word "interbeing." The verb "to be" can be misleading, because we cannot be by ourselves, alone. "To be" is always to "inter-be." If we combine the prefix "inter" with the verb "to be," we have a new verb, "inter-be." To inter-be and the action of interbeing reflects reality more accurately. We inter-are with one another and with all life.

The realizations of emptiness and impermanence are critical ingredients to our own happiness in this life—as well as in the time period approaching our death (the Bardo of This Life), as we die (the Bardo of Dying), and beyond (the Bardo of Luminosity).

Practice Developing Wisdom

Contemplating the impermanent nature of our life, our body, our environment, our friends, our loved ones, and our possessions helps to reduce our grasping nature. The more we are able to reduce our clinging to what is impermanent, the happier our life will be, and the easier our death will be.

Meditation on our breath can help our mind to absorb the impermanence of our world. We can observe our breath as it rises and falls, comes and goes, and changes from one moment to another. A sitting meditation that observes our breath helps develop the realization of emptiness and impermanence.

Observing our breath, and all of its uniqueness, and observing our thoughts passing through our minds helps us to see that everything is always changing. And that's reality, and that's okay.

With eyes closed or looking softly down, spine tall (lying down is okay if sitting is uncomfortable or painful), and body relaxed, we simply observe our natural breathing. As we inhale, we observe the air coming into our body. We can observe the air coming into our nose, or the rise of our abdomen. We can observe the air exiting through our nose or the gentle collapse in our abdomen.

When thoughts come into our mind and interrupt our observation—and they will—we simply go back to observing our breathing, without any judgment whatsoever.

We play this "game" of observing our breath, being interrupted and distracted, and going back to observing our breath. We can start with five minutes a day and gradually, over weeks, increase to fifteen to twenty minutes a day. Maybe even twice a day!

With study, contemplation, and meditation, over time, our mind calms and begins to accept the reality of emptiness and impermanence. We can read books that inspire us and make us think about our lives, their meaning, and our direction in life. We can have conversations with other like-minded individuals. We can spend time digesting the teachings on love and wisdom from the great teachers of any religion.

Change is not bad or good. It just is. It does not mean that everything falls apart for the worst. Inevitable change simply means that everything is possible. As we realize this more and more, we are not surprised by change, and may even enjoy it. Ignorance of this reality is not bliss—only suffering.

Additional practices that we can incorporate into our daily lives to develop our understanding of wisdom are found in appendix A.

How Are Wisdom and Compassion Related?

The more compassionate we become, the more positive karma we accumulate. We are reducing our clinging to who we "think" we are and become more open to the reality of our ever-changing illusory self-identity.

When we recognize that we all want to be happy and suffer as little as possible, we realize we are all the "same." This mindset reduces the "me" versus "other" separateness mentality.

Understanding the interrelated nature of everything is another way of understanding that nothing is permanent. We are connected to each other and dependent upon each other.

Everything changes, and that is okay. This is normal—just like the law of gravity.

Conversely, when we understand impermanence and that everything is interdependent, this can naturally lead to compassion for everyone. We understand that we are all interconnected.

No borders really exist between you and me. There is no dualism. There is no "you" over there and "me" over here, no tribalism. In essence, we can have more of a sense of oneness.

As the Dalai Lama says: "We are all brothers and sisters."

Compassion leads to wisdom, and wisdom leads to compassion. Development of these two key ingredients leads us to a happier life, a more peaceful death, and an auspicious rebirth.

Chapter 6

Supporting Loved Ones as They Approach Death

Our loved ones have lived their lives as best they can, and now their impending death awaits. The past is gone and can't be changed. And the final clock is ticking down. Maybe they believe in the bardo, maybe they don't. We can still help them die peacefully. These suggestions will help them transition to their next phase with less emotional suffering.

Prepare Our State of Mind

Our loved one and those who care about them may be in emotional and/or physical pain. We may be in emotional pain as well. Sometimes the stress of a coming loss drives us to try to control what is going on around us. We may think we know best. And we want to be of help.

Before we can be of help, let's check in with ourselves. Take a few minutes before entering the house, room, or hospital.

How are you doing? What are you feeling? If we can observe and witness our feelings and emotions, we can be more in touch with how we are feeling. There is no need to validate, label, judge, analyze, or suppress any of these emotions. We are just checking in and observing. This alone will help us be centered, calm, and ready to help. One way to check in is to observe your breath for a few minutes.

Now that we have checked in with ourselves, it is good to recognize that we are there to reduce suffering. We may not need to control anything. We can take the attitude of being of service to those who are suffering. We are there to support, to listen, and to be of service. What a beautiful opportunity.

Plan Ahead

Consider bringing a plant, flowers, or pictures that your loved one or people who visit might enjoy. Pictures made by children or grandchildren can bring joy and hope. Light, soft music can lift spirits. Favorite foods, if allowed, can do wonders. Ask beforehand what foods may be appreciated.

Before Entering

Prior to entering the dying person's room or home, we can take a few minutes to check in with ourselves. We can take a few breaths; experience a few moments of silence; recite a prayer or meditation. These will help us bring calm and love to our self and our loved one. In fact, we can do these simple practices any time of day, anywhere. As we develop this habit, it will become natural to do it whenever we need it in any circumstance.

Maintain a Peaceful and Quiet Environment

As our loved ones are dying, they can be very sensitive, and their hearing can be quite good—regardless of their condition. They can likely hear, understand, or feel loud noises from another room, arguments about their condition, or discussions of troubling news. Speaking quietly and calmly can allow them to feel at peace.

Limit or Eliminate Interpersonal Tension

Any differences between family members or friends should be placed on the back burner until after visiting the dying person. Or better yet, now is a good time to mend any fences that may need repair. If the time feels right, requesting and giving forgiveness allows the dying person to let go of life without being pulled back by loose emotional ends. If it doesn't feel right to do so, then we can show that a relationship is one of love and support simply by how we are at any given moment. Not everything needs to be talked out. We can let our love and the look in our eyes express our love and support.

Disagreements with Family Members or Friends

Ask or, if appropriate, maybe encourage the dying person to make up with anyone else they may have had differences with. You can give them the opportunity to voice their sentiments, regrets, or apologies to you—or even in silence. Their prayers and thoughts will be heard. And, of course, if requested, you will share their sentiments with the other party.

Keep Calm

The emotions you experience and exhibit while in the dying person's presence can be felt and can impact their state of mind. If you are calm, they are more likely to be calm. If you are agitated or upset, it will be difficult for them to be calm. Remember, we want to afford them the opportunity to pass in a peaceful state of mind. If it is not possible for you to be calm, then feel free to regroup—step outside the room and take a few moments to breathe and center yourself. Do this as many times as needed. There is no formula for how to stay calm during difficult times. We can only do what we can do at that moment.

Be a Good Listener

Doing our best to accommodate the dying person's wishes is a great act of compassion. If they want to talk, then we can listen intently—without judgment. If they want quiet, we can offer peaceful silence. You can intuit what they might want—or just ask them. Even if they are not speaking, sitting in silence is a beautiful way to support and connect with another human being.

Offer Specifics

You can ask them softly and gently if they want more water, ice chips, medication, food, or their favorite music. No need to bombard them with these questions. You can ask these questions a little at a time—gently and softly.

Get Professional Help

Consider bringing in a professional or religious guide to provide support. There are wonderful hospice workers, death doulas, hospital chaplains, rabbis, priests, and imams who are steeped with wisdom. They are experienced in listening and supporting people near the end of life and their loved ones. They are also likely to know the answers to many questions that may arise. It is good to plan this in advance if possible.

Do Not Push or Pull

Be gentle. No need to pull or push the dying person about any additional loose ends, tasks, or things to think about. Now is not the time for decisions or weighty conversation.

Ensure They Are Physically Comfortable

Pillows, bed adjustments, bed direction, lights, sounds, or where you are sitting can all be sources of comfort or stress. Seek help if it is difficult to physically accommodate your friend or loved one. No rush. All may be done calmly and safely.

Play Music

Music can be helpful to calm the spirit. Offer to play their favorite music on a device, or to sing or play an instrument for them. Sometimes the sound of the human voice in person can make a strong and supportive connection. Ask, or intuit, what might make them feel comfortable.

Offer Specific Prayers or Chants

If you know the dying person has favorite prayers or practices, offer these or seek support in doing so. It is also okay to ask what their preference is in that moment. Honor their wishes with respect and non-judgment. Open mindedness and support are the watchwords of the time.

Support Them with a Spiritual Guide

Hang a picture of their favorite religious figure, saint, or deity (e.g., Jesus, Moses, Buddha, Mary, etc.) or bring other items that may help them feel spiritually connected. If possible, it's good to ask in advance about this. But it is also okay to ask them what their preference is in that moment.

Be Present

Your presence is the greatest gift you can offer someone who is dying. Even if it is uncomfortable for you, it can be deeply meaningful and reassuring. The best way to avoid feeling awkward is just to be present in that moment with your friend or loved one. Your attention is what has the greatest impact. In that vein, it is a good time to turn your phone off.

Observing and connecting with your natural breathing can help you stay present and settle a racing or agitated mind. In the moment you are with a loved one, there is no need to think about what you can, or should, do or say—offering the care of your attention is more than sufficient.

Let It Be

Regardless of their state of mind, we can be open and understanding. Most people are not prepared for dying. We can listen. Be present. Be calm.

If the dying person is agitated, listen quietly. Your calm, soft demeanor is likely to calm them. We cannot control their state of mind—we can only offer ours. Sometimes even just offering your hand in theirs can have a calming effect.

What May Arise During the Visit?

Your loved one can be experiencing fear, uncertainty, anger, guilt, regret, depression, and a whole host of spiraling emotions.

If they want to hear your perspective, you can speak with a calm and reassuring tone and share:

- how they have done wonderful things in their life
- how their belief in God or other Higher Being will take care of them when they pass
- that you will of course miss them. And you will remember all the wonderful memories you have, what you have learned, and what you will be able to pass onto others
- how their lives have impacted others for the better
- how much you or others have loved and cherished them

- how their presence in the world will live on through others, for generations to come

Your loved one may appear not to be conscious of visitors or their surroundings, but please don't let that stop you from sharing words of care and encouragement.

Science has proven that people who are dying, or comatose, may in fact hear what is being said around them. With that in mind, we can still speak with them calmly, and express our love or respect or admiration for them.

How Do You Handle Questions about Death or Beyond?

If your loved one expresses anxiety about death or what comes next, you can assure your loved one that:

- God, or the Higher Presence that they believe in, is one of forgiveness and acceptance—and they can count on that
- they can focus on their God, or a Higher Power, that is always with them. That focus alone is enough to be welcomed into heaven, the kingdom of God, the afterlife, or the bardo
- without any doubt their love, positive deeds, and thoughts will do them well as they enter the next phase

Repeating prayers or mantras, out loud or silently, will help them stay connected with God or that Higher Being. A mantra is a phrase or word whose sound and/or meaning resonates to help with concentration, or to clarify and purify our state of mind. Each faith has its own phrases that can bring solace and comfort.

Christ, Mary, Buddha, the Prophet Mohammad, and Moses are all representations and manifestations of love, compassion—a Higher Being. They can be relied on to hear anyone's call for help or compassion. Your loved one can be encouraged to speak with these wonderful Higher Beings, or pray to them. In appendix A we offer words of encouragement that might help in this way.

How Can We Recognize the Signs of Death?

When we are attentive and our minds are clear, with some experience, we are able to see and feel the progression of the physical body shutting down. By studying what is going on in the body when it goes through the dying process, we will not be surprised as it happens. We can gain confidence or mental comfort as we follow this progression as it happens in others or ourselves. We can recite the appropriate prayers before death, if that is part of our practice, and know when it is time to remove the body after death.

By observing this progression, we can know if death is near or still far off. Tibetan medicine has detailed the signs of the body's deterioration. They mirror closely to Western observations.

The following is a brief overview of the major signs that accompany the dying process:

PHASE 1

The body feels weak, and as though it is sinking into the earth. Eyes can't stay open, and the body's color is dull.

PHASE 2

The body feels dry, and one may feel very thirsty. The hearing sense is diminished.

PHASE 3

Digestion is difficult. Memory fades. Inhalation is weak, while exhalation becomes relatively stronger. Smell is diminished or gone.

PHASE 4

Awareness of what is going on around us is reduced. Taste is reduced or gone. Touch sense is lessened.

PHASE 5

Gross consciousness ceases. Our perceptions, cognition, sense of self, personality all cease. Subtle consciousness remains—a feeling of timelessness, unbounded love, being at one with all.

PHASES 6–8

A practitioner may become more aware of their heart chakra, an energy center located at the center of the chest at heart level.

Depending upon one's preparation, the mind's awareness may experience a state of clear light or the true nature of reality (for details, please see appendix B, The Tibetan Book of the Dead—A Summary).

Consciousness leaves the body, which can be noted when the heart center is no longer warm. The body begins to smell as it decomposes. The observer has a subtle sense that the consciousness has left.

It is at this point, when consciousness leaves the body, that traditional Buddhist lamas recite prayers and have the body removed. In the absence of experienced lamas, you may recite the prayers in next chapter.

While these phases of dying are common, each person and progression of death is different. The most important points are—be present, be calm, be kind, listen with your entire being, be of service. That is the best way to show our love and support.

Chapter 7

Practices as Death Approaches

Buddhists from Tibetan lineages practice Phowa, a combination of visualization and mantra that merges their consciousness with a Higher Being at the end of life.

Phowa can be traced back to the great Buddhist Master Tilopa from the eleventh century and his teacher Sukhasiddhi, a female Indian teacher of Vajrayana Buddhism, a yogini and master of meditation. It is likely that she learned Phowa from teachers or primordial Buddhas who preceded her. Since that time many Tibetan Buddhist lineages have developed their own flavor of Phowa practice.

Performing Phowa while dying reduces the burden of negative karma that the practitioner has accumulated through their lifetime(s). The abbreviated Phowa practice in this chapter, along with practices provided in appendix A, can be of tremendous benefit for anyone of any religion.

When Phowa is performed with sincerity and surrender, the dying practitioner will have an auspicious rebirth in their next lifetime on earth. The dying practitioner who practices Phowa may have the option of attaining rebirth in a Pure Land. A Pure Land is a land of beauty that exceeds all other worlds or realms that one can be reborn into. Being reborn into a Pure Land is equivalent to becoming enlightened. In that case, their consciousness would not be reborn in the world we currently live in.

Lamas from Tibetan Buddhist lineages may lead their dying students through the Phowa practice to help them attain an auspicious rebirth in the human realm, to reach the Pure Land, or to achieve enlightenment.

Dying Buddhist practitioners—as well as non-Buddhists—can practice a simplified, but effective, version of Phowa for themselves. We don't have to wait until death to connect our mind with a Higher Being. And you can lead your loved one through a version of Phowa practice, as well. The practice helps them to release grasping (negative karma) and unite their consciousness with a Higher Being.

If our loved ones are open to it, let them know you will lead them through a transformative, peaceful, and loving practice that may ease their suffering and help them pass peacefully. It can be practiced by anyone, from any religious faith or background. It will help them connect with their Higher Being, God, or Higher Power.

Phowa may be practiced during the last living hours. We can guide them by reciting a short version of Phowa, provided below, with a soft, loving, and calm voice. Traditionally, it is recited with the guide sitting next to the loved one's head—not near their feet.

After we guide them several times, our loved one can practice this on their own. Many people practice Phowa themselves, even if death is not approaching. It is a wonderful way to connect with a Higher Being.

In addition to Phowa, at the moment of death, we can also provide gentle encouragement to guide them on to the bardo, or world beyond. The encouragement will help them move forward, instead of clinging to their body or old life.

Here are examples of an Abbreviated Phowa Visualization and Encouragement that we can recite to the dying person softly and slowly. If possible, sit physically close to them, and speak slowly and quietly into their ear.

Read the next section, filling in the Higher Presence or Supreme Being that they most relate to. If you don't know, it is okay to ask them who that Higher Being might be: Jesus, Moses, Buddha, Mary, Mohammed, and so on.

Abbreviated Phowa Visualization

This brief Phowa practice can be very impactful. You are welcome to modify it as feels right for the dying person or for yourself. Read the following:

> Gently close your eyes and let's observe our breath for a few minutes.

> Don't worry about any distracting thoughts or sounds that you may hear.

> When you notice you are distracted, no problem. Just go back to observing your natural and unique breathing.

Observe the air coming in and out of your nostrils, or the rise and fall of your abdomen or chest. Just watch, and appreciate the breathing that has been your friend all of your life.

[Pause to allow them to observe their breath.]

Imagine that your most precious God, Higher Presence, or Golden Light is in the room.

It could be any Higher Being for whom you feel love or great respect, devotion, or connection.

It does not matter whether or not you have had this connection during your lifetime. Now is all that matters.

We will be able to invoke their presence now.

[NAME OF HIGHER BEING here and in the blanks that follow: _____] has been with you all of your life, and now [he/she/they] is making [himself/herself/themself] known to you.

Now is the time for you to imagine that [_____] is connected to your heart. [_____] has come to keep you company.

Imagine that [_____] is present in the form of a white light. That is all you need to feel now.

The warmth of the white light is around your head and flows from their heart into your heart. [_____]'s presence is calm and loving toward you.

You can feel [him/her/them]. And you can feel your sense of devotion to [him/her/them] coming from your heart.

[_____] is so happy to be with you and see you.

[_____] can feel your essence and you are very beautiful to [him/her/them].

[_____] is smiling at you and is so happy and appreciates you so much.

Take a few moments, or as long as you wish, so you can take in and feel their presence, and their white light.

It does not need to be any specific visualization; just a warm, loving sense of light.

[Pause to allow them to observe.]

[_____] has come to you to welcome you to your next phase.

Now, feel a similar light present in your heart center.

You, too, possess the same white light inside your heart center.

Take your time to appreciate and welcome this moment and this feeling.

After you feel the same essence inside of you, feel a connection between your heart center and this beautiful Higher Being that is your guide, protector, and loving presence.

Feel the connection. Now feel yourself and [_____] merge together into one essence.

You are coming home to be with them. They are so happy to be with you and welcome you.

Rest in that feeling for as long as you like.

Take your time. There is no rush. Repeat this whenever you would like.

Encouragement

The following may be recited slowly and softly during the last moments of life. It is based on the teachings of Guru Padmasambhava, the originator of the teachings in *The Tibetan Book of the Dead*. Please feel free to modify as you see fit.

[Loved One's Name: _____]

Do not be afraid. You are surrounded by love.

You have now arrived at the moment of death.

There is no turning back.

This is the natural state of the cycle of life for all living things.

Go forward to the [world beyond | the bardo].

Do not cling to the present life.

No need to grasp or be attached to your previous life.

The body has expired.

It is time to move forward.

Take refuge in the presence of [NAME OF HIGHER BEING: _____]

[Repeat the above several times and repeat the last line several times.]

Chapter 8

Supporting Dying Loved Ones from a Distance

W e can hold a loved one in mind—regardless of distance. It matters not where our friend, family member, or loved one is. We can feel them. In our mind, we can see them. We can participate in any of these practices, prayers, or visualizations— wherever we are and wherever they are.

We are all connected. We all affect one another—whether you feel it or not. When we look around and see all the numerous causes that create numerous consequences, we can't ignore that we are all connected.

The COVID-19 pandemic illustrated that we are no longer billions of individuals doing our own thing. We never were. We are not 195 countries existing independently in this world. The pandemic went from one person to the next, infecting more than 560 million people around the world as we wrote this book. Yes, we are all connected.

Suffering and love also travel the distance. We can feel pain around the world. The images of sorrow flashed around the world on TV, news, or Internet make the feelings even more palpable. We can also feel love and relief for those who survive.

Many of us survived. Many of us helped others. Many countries supported individuals from countries on the other side of the world. There was a realization that we are all in this together. In a pandemic or not, this interconnection and interbeing always exists.

Supporting Loved Ones from a Distance

We can pray, chant, or visualize with our loved ones, even if they are far away. Do so as if your loved one is right next to you. They are. If you have any doubt, try it and see what you feel. Practice the Phowa and the Encouragement in the previous chapter. Your loved one is close by.

Prepare an environment that is conducive to the practices described in this book. A clean, sacred, thoughtful area or room can be prepared for meditation, visualization, singing, and praying. Candles, incense, and beautiful pictures can adorn the room. A picture of our loved one can be placed next to images of holy beings that inspire us.

To feel closer, you can, of course, talk to them by phone or video. You, or your children, can create and send artwork or music. Show appreciation and love. Always be open, sensitive, and non-judgmental with a positive mentality of service and support.

And finally, let's give the support and love with all that we have—through our devotion and surrender to God or a Higher Being. God or a Higher Being can continue to support you and your loved one as they pass through their death.

Chapter 9

Supporting Ourselves
at the End of Life

What has passed in this life is ancient history. You are now at the threshold of a beautiful, wondrous, and new opportunity.

Death is just as natural as birth. Death is not to be feared. It can be viewed as an opportunity to connect with God, or a higher being. We need to come to a place in our mind where we can accept this.

Focus on the "prize"—a beautiful transition to the next phase in the cycle of birth-life-death—and do not be distracted by doubts or fears. Through meditation we can learn to stay focused on what is happening now. It's as simple as observing your breath for a few minutes at a time. No fancy instruction is needed. This retrains our mind to stay in the present moment— no need to review the past or worry about the future.

Let's not create illusions in our mind.

Reality is that our sense of "self" is an illusion.

Reality is everything and is always changing.

Reality is we die, and we go to an afterlife of one kind or another.

Whether you believe in an afterlife or not, why not make your death a celebration?

Why not love yourself like you never have?

Why not encourage your loved ones to support you in the most positive, joyful way they know how?

If you believe that your death is weeks or months away, please practice the prayers and chants on Compassion and Wisdom shared in chapter 5—reciting the Four Immeasurables and meditating on your breath. Please establish a consistent meditation practice for yourself.

If you can't do it on your own, find a teacher who is supportive.

Feeling stressed? Observe your breath. It will keep you in the present moment.

"The past is history. The future is mystery. The present moment is a gift."

Chapter 10

The Time Immediately after Death

When a loved one has passed and is no longer breathing, or when death has been verified, being calm, aware, and loving can continue to support their consciousness.

From those who have died and returned to their body in a near-death experience, we know that in many cases the deceased can still "hear" what is going on. The consciousness may still be aware and very sensitive, even after death.

For example, agitated crying can still be "heard" and sensed by the deceased. It can impact the deceased's consciousness as they continue through the bardo.

If this emotion can't be avoided, then best for the bereaved to leave the room until they have calmed down.

Buddhists may leave a body in place, at rest, for a period of time. This is done, once again, to give the consciousness time to acclimate to the bardo with calmness, and to allow Buddhist priests or lamas to pray and guide the consciousness.

Followers of Tibetan Buddhist schools may leave a body in its place for up to seven days, according to astrological charts.

Pure Land Buddhists leave a body at rest for twelve to twenty-four hours. The specifics of the practice are different, but the overall intent to allow the body to rest and the consciousness to move on in peace are consistent.

Given the practicality and laws of the country, leaving a body in place for lengthy time periods may not be possible. Best to plan in advance for what is practical and possible. Many leave the body at rest for a few hours. The length of time is not the key factor—how the time is spent during that rest period is of greater importance.

While the body is at rest, prayers can be read, poetry can be recited, and gentle soft music can be played. It is also very calming and beautiful to have butter lamps or candles lit.

Calm, joyful thoughts about the individual can help both the bereaved and the deceased. Positive thoughts, speech, and actions after death can all help the consciousness acclimate and move on through the bardo in a calm state.

It is our opportunity to wish our loved one peace on their journey, and to encourage their consciousness to move on peacefully to their next phase after death.

Days or weeks later, consider a celebration event of the deceased's life. Joy and tears can mix in a celebration of how that person was able to be of benefit to others in their lives.

Celebration activities can include donating to a cause important to the deceased, planting a tree in their honor, or performing a Life Release.

Life Release is a traditional Buddhist practice of saving the lives of beings that were destined for slaughter. It can include purchasing, and then releasing, any animal that was slated for slaughter—for example, fish, crickets, grasshoppers—back into their natural habitat, to be free from being killed.

All activities to benefit others are dedicated to the life of the deceased. This merit will help their consciousness, improve their karma as they navigate the bardo, or move on to their next phase after life.

Chapter 11

Essential Advice for Joyful Living and Peaceful Dying

Since how we live is how we die, we offer these reflections for courageous living.

We hope you find them helpful and inspiring.

Peace in Our Mind

What we see, what we hear, what we feel—they are all reflections of our mind.

If we are in a good state of mind, we can see the beauty in what is around us. We can appreciate the things and people in our life. If we are not in a good state of mind, then everything around us is insufficient and lacking.

When we understand our mind, we understand all of life.

We can't change others. We can only change our "self."

If we want peace in our lives, then we need to find the peace in our "self."

Learn to meditate to be able to live in peace and live in reality without illusion.

The best way to prepare for death is to live a simple life and enjoy it. The less we have, the fewer problems we will experience. Chasing possessions, or money, will not bring happiness. Let go of unnecessary material things and petty grievances.

Practical Planning

We can prepare for death and show care for our loved ones by getting our material and financial affairs in order. This avoids arguments after we are gone. Create a will.

Talk with family members about the dying process, how you feel, and what you would like when the time comes.

Put in writing how family or friends can help during the dying process or after death.

Success and Appreciation

Real success is when we have peace in our home and happiness in our heart. Then we are truly a successful person.

The richest people in the world are still chasing and purchasing things and businesses. Are they enjoying life? Are they satisfied, or do they still want to buy more?

We can have material things, but the real key is to enjoy what we have—now.

If we are rich, it is wonderful because we can share and give to help others.

Many of us live in abundance. We need to appreciate it and enjoy it. Enjoy the weather. Enjoy our family. Enjoy our life. It doesn't matter if we are rich or poor—enjoy.

If we want to be happy, we need to train ourselves to appreciate what we do have. No need to pine or grasp for what we don't have.

When we appreciate our life, there is no suffering.

Daily Life

When you wake up, create a beautiful motivation for the day. "I am going to enjoy my work. I am so glad I have a place to sleep. I am glad I have a job to work. I am glad I have a family."

Eat healthfully. Exercise. Speak with your doctor or nutritionist and find out what is best for you. Listen to your body—and learn what is good for you and not good for you.

Depression or Anxiety

Don't be afraid to seek professional support—psychological or spiritual. We are all "works in progress" and having a professional at our side can be very helpful and comforting. We can't possibly know everything or know how to heal ourselves in every situation. That is what the experts are for!

Life and death are both an adventure. Prepare and be positive.

Appendix A

Practices to Develop Compassion and Wisdom

A s discussed in chapter 5, the development of Compassion and Wisdom leads us to a happier life, a peaceful death, and an auspicious rebirth. Here are additional practices to cultivate compassion and wisdom in our lives.

Practice to Develop Compassion:
Lovingkindness Meditation

"If you want others to be happy,
practice compassion.
If you want to be happy, practice compassion."

—HIS HOLINESS THE 14TH DALAI LAMA

Take a few minutes to sit peacefully with your eyes closed
or looking down and observe your breath as you breathe
in and out.

Allow yourself to breathe naturally, without any modification of the breath.

For a few minutes, simply observe your breath in its
most natural state, as it passes through your nostrils.

If you find that you are distracted by your thoughts or
sounds, no problem; just go back to observing your breath.

Part 1

When you are calm, recite the following verse to yourself
three times, slowly with intention and devotion:

May I be happy.
May I be peaceful.
May I be free from suffering.

Now observe your breath, as you did earlier, for a few
moments.

Part 2

Keeping in mind a loved one or a family member, recite the following verse three times, filling in the loved one's name, slowly with intention and devotion:

> May [fill in the name] be happy.
> May [fill in the name] be peaceful.
> May [fill in the name] be free from suffering.

Now observe your breath, as you did earlier, for a few moments.

Part 3

Keeping in mind someone you feel neutral about (e.g., the cashier at the grocery store, or someone you don't know that well), recite the verse three times and fill in the person's name. If you don't know their name, it is okay to use a descriptive title (e.g., bank teller):

> May [fill in the name] be happy.
> May [fill in the name] be peaceful.
> May [fill in the name] be free from suffering.

Now observe your breath, as you did earlier, for a few moments.

Part 4

Bring to mind someone you have difficulty with (e.g., someone you don't care for or find annoying). Recite the verse three times and fill in the person's name:

> May [fill in the name] be happy.
> May [fill in the name] be peaceful.
> May [fill in the name] be free from suffering.

Now observe your breath, as you did earlier, for a few moments.

When done, express to a Higher Being, your teacher, or your higher self a sense of gratitude that you have the ability to practice compassion for yourself and others.

Practicing lovingkindness might feel simple, but it can be deeply transformative. It has been taught by centuries of Buddhist teachers, and it works in these ways:

- When we focus on our breath, we are in the moment.
- Being in the moment automatically stops any habitual thinking about the past and the future.
- When we help others, we feel better.
- When we help ourselves, we feel better.
- We are transforming the negative state of mind into a positive one.
- This trains us to be able to change our state of mind quickly.
- This meditation reduces the attachment to anger—or whatever negative state of mind is being experienced.

- It allows our mind to be more malleable and shows us that our thoughts and emotions are ephemeral.

Practice to Develop Wisdom:
Observation Meditation

"If you wish to make an apple pie from
scratch, you must first invent the universe."

—CARL SAGAN, COSMOLOGIST

We can use analytical meditation to develop wisdom that
helps us understand the "emptiness of all phenomena,"
and the reality of our "self."

The emptiness of all phenomena means simply that
our reality is always changing. Nothing is solid and
permanent.

By understanding this, and reminding ourselves that
everything is always changing, it helps us reduce our
grasping and clinging to things that we think are solid
and permanent—people, places, and experiences.

The grasping and clinging is what causes us suffering.

We typically also view our "self" as a solid, permanent being. And, as a result, this makes it difficult for us
to be flexible and see others and ourselves with an open
mind—without judgment.

We have a view of who we are that is quite fixed—our
self-identity. This identity is developed and supported by
the stories we tell ourselves, about who we think we are.
And when something happens that threatens that view,
we can get angry, annoyed, or fearful.

By understanding that we are always changing, and
that our "self" doesn't exist in a permanent sense, we
can be more flexible with our views of ourselves, others,

situations, and expectations. We can be more understanding of other people and situations.

Realizing Emptiness and Connection

Take a few minutes to sit peacefully with your eyes closed or looking down. Observe your breath as you breathe in and out.

Allow yourself to breathe naturally, without any modification of the breath.

For a few minutes, simply observe your breath in its most natural state, as it passes through your nostrils.

If you find that you are distracted by your thoughts or sounds, no problem; just go back to observing your breath.

In your mind, see a table.

In English, it is described by the word "table."

This table is made up of many pieces: a top, legs, glue, nails, and varnish.

The legs and top are made up of wood from a tree. Before the tree was cut down it grew as a result of many variables—sunlight, seeds, rain, earth, and wind, to name just a few.

And before it was a tree, it was a seed from another tree, and another tree before that.

What about the nails or the varnish? Those items can also be traced backward to the people, companies, and components that went into their production.

And the people who created the components also came into being from their parents, and their parents before them.

We now see that everything around us—all phenomena—were caused by something that preceded it and can be traced back to a beginningless time.

Next time, pick another thing, place, or person and go through the same logic. As you go about your day, notice everything around you and apply the same logic.

When you walk around your work or home environment, notice that everything is empty of inherent existence. Everything has a name that refers to a thing that comes together for a time.

Zen teacher Norman Fischer said:

In the end everything is just designation: things have a kind of reality in their being named and conceptualized, but otherwise they actually aren't there in the way we think they are.

That is, connection is all you find, with no things that are connected.[. . .] It's the very thoroughness of the connection—without gaps or lumps in it—only the constant nexus wherever you turn—that renders everything void. So everything is empty and connected or empty because connected. Emptiness is connection.

No Solid Self

Take a few minutes to sit peacefully with your eyes closed or looking down. Observe your breath as you breathe in and out.

Allow yourself to breathe naturally, without any modification of the breath.

For a few minutes simply observe your breath in its most natural state, as it passes through your nostrils.

If you find that you are distracted by your thoughts or sounds, no problem; just go back to observing your breath.

Read the following and then contemplate each question one at a time:

- Can you identify and define your "self?" Where is it? Can you show it to someone? Is it fixed? Is it permanent?

Close your eyes and contemplate this for a few minutes.

- Are the opinions and views you have of yourself different now than yesterday or a year ago?

Close your eyes and contemplate this for a few minutes.

- What about other people—are they growing or dying—and changing along the way? Might their views, opinions, and motivations be changing too?

Close your eyes and contemplate this for a few minutes.

- Consider that we are always changing, and our views of our "selves" and others are based on an illusion of permanence. The illusion is that we think that our views, and what is around us, are solid and permanent. This is not true.

Close your eyes and contemplate this for a few minutes.

- Thoughts, views, feelings, opinions, motivation, and judgment are subject to change from moment to moment—ours and everyone else's. As a result, we would be foolish to judge anyone's motivation, or even trust our own views with great certainty.

  As we contemplate this more and more, we will understand that "reality" is not what we think it is. It is something more nuanced, always changing, and more illusory than we think.

  We can be more open-minded to the views of those around us, and more compassionate to our "selves" and others.

Close your eyes and contemplate this for a few minutes. May all beings benefit.

Appendix B

The Tibetan Book of the Dead—A Summary

The Tibetan Book of the Dead, composed in the eighth century by the great Buddhist Master Padmasambhava, describes instructions that an accomplished Buddhist lama uses to guide the dying Buddhist practitioner to liberation, or through the bardos (the post-death states of consciousness) to an auspicious rebirth.

These instructions are also meant to be employed while we are alive and healthy, as part of our daily Buddhist practice. They prepare us to approach death and the bardos and are a road map to liberation.

The Tibetan Book of the Dead in the Tibetan language is called *Bardo Thodol.* The direct translation of *Bardo Thodol* is *Liberation Through Hearing in the Intermediate State.*

Why hearing?

Qualified Buddhist lamas instruct the dying individual by whispering or chanting these prayers, or visualizations, melodiously into their ear.

The lama has practiced these esoteric, powerful, and effective practices for many years, if not lifetimes. In turn, the dying person has ideally practiced these prayers and visualizations throughout their lifetime and, more importantly, developed great devotion and trust in the lama, who is often their Buddhist teacher.

The lama is motivated to help reduce suffering of sentient beings. With that strong mindset, the lama guides the dying person to liberation, or to rebirth.

The Tibetan Book of the Dead is read, or recited, by the lama, and sometimes with monks who join in support of the dying individual. The practices include:

- a description of the six bardos that make up the birth-life-death cycle
- an introduction to the ultimate nature of our mind. This phrase can be described as Buddha nature, the primordial aspect of all sentient beings. Other descriptions are the realization of the emptiness of all phenomena, or the mind that is primordial and radiant (all aware).

In *The Great Medicine That Conquers Clinging to the Notion of Reality: Steps in Meditation on the Enlightened Mind*, Shechen Rabjam (1871–1926), a principal lineage holder in Tibetan Buddhism, describes Buddha nature as follows: "Buddha nature is immaculate. It is profound, serene, unfabricated suchness, an uncompounded expanse of luminosity; nonarising, unceasing, primordial peace, spontaneously present nirvana."

- a practice where the dying person develops an awareness of the different aspects of their mind
- a practice for the dying person to help them recognize that everything they see and experience is a reflection of their mind
- a prostration practice, where prostrations are performed while visualizing Buddhist deities (emanations of enlightened beings) in front of them. The visualization of, and devotion to, these magnificent deities allow the practitioner to purify their own karma through confession and expressions of regret for the negative habits they developed during their lifetime
- a prayer practice where the dying person confesses their negative karma and resolves not to repeat the actions that caused it
- a description of how and when the body degrades as it approaches death. This allows the qualified Buddhist lama to guide the dying person through the practices described here, based on the stages of dying that are taking place
- a practice that transfers consciousness (negative karma) to a higher being as one dies. By reducing or eliminating negative karma in this way, the dying person can proceed through the bardo to rebirth without the burden of negative karma
- a protocol where the lama can free the dying person from the suffering that all beings experience as they go through cyclic existence (i.e., birth-life-death)

- visualization and recitation practices that help the dying person merge their mind with the mind of enlightenment
- refuge prayers where the dying person expresses their devotion to the Three Jewels of Buddhism—the Buddha, the Dharma, and the Sangha
- refuge prayers where the dying person expresses their devotion to the buddhas and bodhisattvas

For traditional Buddhist practitioners of Tibetan lineages, these prayers and protocols are chanted to the dying person over many weeks, as they go through the Bardo of Dying and the Bardo of Luminosity.

May all beings benefit.

Resources

Books

The Five Invitations: Discovering What Death Can Teach Us About Living Fully by Frank Ostaseski

How We Live is How We Die by Pema Chödrön

Graceful Exits: How Great Beings Die by Sushila Blackman

Preparing to Die by Andrew Holecek

Peaceful Death, Joyful Rebirth by Tulku Thondup

Movies

Groundhog Day (Dir. Harold Ramis, 1993)

The Sixth Sense (Dir. M. Night Shyamalan, 1999)

Defending Your Life (Dir. Albert Brooks, 1991)

Ghost (Dir. Jerry Zucker, 1990)

I Origins (Dir. Mike Cahill, 2014)

Meditation

Meditation Pro Series by Mordy Levine (Spotify)

Insight Timer (app)

Ten Percent Happier (app)

Thoughts About Rebirth

University of Virginia School of Medicine (Division of Perceptual Studies) has scientifically documented over twenty-five hundred cases of children, from families of all religions, who have recalled their previous lives in great detail. Their scientists and researchers are tasked with identifying and validating any claims of rebirth or reincarnation. med.virginia.edu/perceptual-studies.

"The Buddhist Teachings on Rebirth," *Lion's Roar Magazine* (May 12, 2018). lionsroar.com/just-more-of-the-same.

Sam Littlefair, "Do You Only Live Once? The Evidence for Rebirth," *Lion's Roar Magazine* (May 11, 2018). lionsroar.com/do-you-only-live-once.

About the Authors

Lama Lhanang

Venerable Lama Lhanang Rinpoche was born in Golok, Amdo, northeast of Tibet. As a child, he entered the Thubten Chokor Ling Monastery located in the Gadê region, Golok, under the guidance of his root teacher Kyabye Orgyen Kusum Lingpa, where in addition to developing a complete monastic education, he trained in the yogi lineage of Anu Yoga.

He was recognized as the rebirth of Khen Rinpoche Damcho, an emanation of Nubchen Namke Nyingpo—one of the twenty-five disciples of Guru Rinpoche—by the Sang Long Monastery located in eastern Tibet.

He has received teachings from a large number of teachers from the different schools and lineages of Tibetan Buddhism, such as His Holiness the 14th Dalai Lama, 4th Dodrupchen Rinpoche, and Kyabye Katok Getse Rinpoche, among others.

Lama Lhanang Rinpoche is a teacher of Vajrayana Buddhism, from the Nyingma school of the Longchen Nyingthig lineage. In addition to the instructions of Buddhism, he studied history, astrology, grammar, Tibetan medicine, painting, sculpture, music, and theater. All this has led him to share teachings on the proper use of the body, the word, and the mind, with the motto: *world peace through inner peace.*

His life in the West has also been dedicated to sharing the teachings of the Buddha through his painting, in which he reflects his relationship with everyday life, no matter where he is in the world.

He currently lives in San Diego, California, with his wife and child. He directs Jigme Lingpa Center in addition to sharing his teachings in centers in the US, Canada, Europe, and Mexico.

Mordy Levine

Mordy Levine has been a Buddhist practitioner for over forty years. He is the creator of the *Meditation Pro Series* that teaches meditation for different conditions that affect Western civilization (e.g., stress, insomnia, weight issues, smoking). To date, over 250 thousand people have learned to meditate through his series of meditation programs. Mordy is the president of Jigme Lingpa Center, a nonprofit organization led by Lama Lhanang Rinpoche. The center's goal is to generate benefit to all beings through the dissemination of the Buddha's teachings of wisdom and compassion in order to achieve a sustainable future of peace and harmony for all. Mordy has been practicing yoga and martial arts for forty years—almost daily. He also meditates daily and holds instructor certifications in karate, Tai Chi, and yoga.

Mordy graduated from Brandeis University with a BA. He attended University of Chicago Business School and graduated with an MBA.

Mordy and his wife, Elizabeth, have a son and live in Rancho Santa Fe with many dogs.

About Sounds True

Sounds True is a multimedia publisher whose mission is to inspire and support personal transformation and spiritual awakening. Founded in 1985 and located in Boulder, Colorado, we work with many of the leading spiritual teachers, thinkers, healers, and visionary artists of our time. We strive with every title to preserve the essential "living wisdom" of the author or artist. It is our goal to create products that not only provide information to a reader or listener but also embody the quality of a wisdom transmission.

For those seeking genuine transformation, Sounds True is your trusted partner. At SoundsTrue.com you will find a wealth of free resources to support your journey, including exclusive weekly audio interviews, free downloads, interactive learning tools, and other special savings on all our titles.

To learn more, please visit SoundsTrue.com/freegifts or call us toll-free at 800.333.9185.